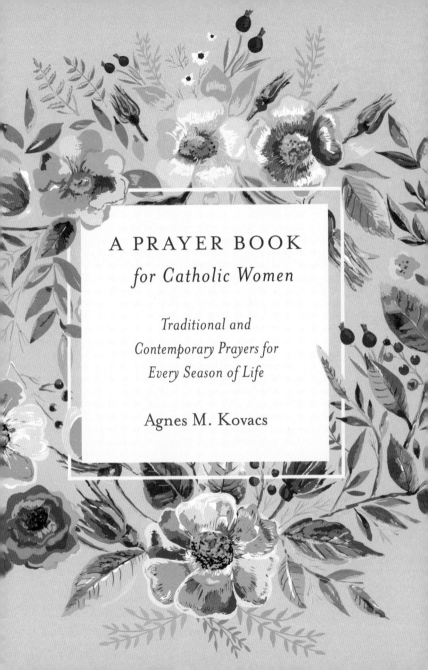

A PRAYER BOOK
for Catholic Women

*Traditional and
Contemporary Prayers for
Every Season of Life*

Agnes M. Kovacs

Published by The Word Among Us Press
7115 Guilford Drive, Suite 100
Frederick, Maryland 21704
wau.org

22 21 20 19 18   1 2 3 4 5

ISBN: 978-1-59325-334-9
eISBN: 978-1-59325-509-1

Compiled by Agnes Kovacs

Cover design by Faceout Studios

Library of Congress Control Number: 2018936171

CONTENTS

INTRODUCTION

"Teach us to pray," we ask, as did the disciples of old. Yet prayer is more an attitude than a skill. It is more about our willingness to do it and less about how we go about it. Some guidance certainly helps, but it is important to know that there is no one right way to pray. Our prayer and prayer life will look different from that of others, depending on our personality, life experiences, and circumstances. And we may find that what once fit beautifully does not appeal anymore, for we have changed. Prayer changes us and changes with us. Prayer is an expression of our need to be in relationship with divine Love, here and now. Saint Augustine said it best: "Our heart is restless until it rests in you."

This book is intended to be a prayer primer: an introduction to prayer and different prayer forms, and an invitation to go deeper. It is more about exploring the territory than about prescribing a concrete direction. It will offer ways to help you nourish your relationship with God and others.

The selection of prayers represents but a small sampling from the bounty of traditional and liturgical prayers of the Church. I have included contemporary compositions by various authors and have identified those throughout the book. I have also written many prayers specifically for this book, and those prayers in Part One that are not identified as traditional or by another author are my compositions.

The content of Part One is organized around seasons—seasons of nature, life, and the spiritual journey—ever mindful of the fact that in different times of our lives, we might find ourselves in different seasons. Part Two contains many traditional prayers of the Church that have helped people, through the ages, as they journeyed through their own seasons. There are also some contemporary prayers; most of these include the name of the author.

May this prayer book serve you well in finding rest in God!

PART ONE

Seasons of Prayer

Chapter One

RESPONDING TO THE DIVINE

Prayer is integral to our Judeo-Christian heritage. Scripture reveals the Hebrew people as steeped in prayer. An entire book, The Book of Psalms, is dedicated to prayer. The Gospel accounts are full of references to Jesus praying. He prayed by himself and with others, in private and in front of thousands. He recited prayers from his Jewish heritage and offered his own. Prayer enabled Jesus to stay in tune with God the Father and gain strength for living his mission.

Liturgical and non-liturgical prayers of the disciples and the early Church were preserved and handed down through the centuries in historical documents such as the writings of the Church Fathers. Prayer is our sure way to connect to God who created us and is drawing us into the divine life.

Prayer can be a prelude to action or a response to unfolding events. Prayer is communication, with or without words.

Prayer is both listening to and responding to God's invitation to be in relationship. Most of all, prayer is a state of being present to God.

Prayer is like a well-made tapestry that is tightly woven from yarns of different colors and types. The variation in these prayer threads creates an image, fosters multisensory engagement, and evokes a response.

Prayer comes in many forms and modes. Prayer can be communal or personal, verbal or silent, and it can involve movement, music, or stillness. It may rely on engagement with nature or emerge from the act of thinking; it may be the fruit of encountering others or going deep within ourselves. Prayer can be formulaic or freely composed; it may spring forth from memory, like prayers we know by heart, or it may be a new particular response to the moment.

Prayer is as varied as human beings are diverse. Whether we use silence, words, movement, music, the visual arts, or any combination thereof, prayer is an expression of our relationship with God.

3

A Prayer Practicum

Praying Spontaneously

Many Catholics find praying spontaneously in a group setting quite intimidating. They worry about finding the right words and putting them together to form a coherent prayer. While God surely sees what is in our hearts, it helps to have a few tools for expressing ourselves.

One formula that may ease anxiety about creating a prayer is ACTS.

A—adoration: "Almighty God, you are . . ."
C—contrition: "I am sorry for . . ."
T—thanksgiving: "Thank you for . . ."
S—supplication: "I ask . . ."

Another formula follows the shape of the Collect prayers of the Mass: You-Who-Do-Through.

You—Name God

Who—Describe what God has done in the past

Do—Ask for God's action now

Through—Finish with the Trinitarian formula: "Grant this through our Lord Jesus Christ, your Son, who lives and reigns with you and the Holy Spirit, now and forever. Amen." Or "We ask this in the name of your beloved Son, Jesus, in the power of the Holy Spirit, one God for ever and ever. Amen."

With some practice, these formulas will become second nature and will enable us to offer prayers under any circumstances.

In our personal prayer, we do not need to use formulas. We can talk to God as if to a friend, sharing our daily joys and struggles without keeping to a set pattern. Many of the prayers that follow fall into this category. Keep in mind that they represent only one side of the conversation that is prayer.

Praying with Scripture

Our common, or public prayer in the liturgy—both the Mass and the Liturgy of the Hours—is deeply scriptural. Listening to the biblical readings proclaimed within liturgy is an essential way to engage with Scripture.

Catholics may feel less comfortable praying with Scripture on their own. But the importance of praying with the Bible gained new momentum after the Second Vatican Council, and we are now encouraged to incorporate Scripture into our personal prayer.

Lectio divina (sacred reading) is an ancient prayer tradition of the Church that is centered on the slow, contemplative reading of a passage from Scripture. If you choose to pray in this manner, these questions should guide your prayer as you slowly read, several times, the selected Scripture passage:

- What does the text say?

- What does the text say to me? How does the text speak to my daily life?

- What do I want to say to God about this text? In light of its relevance for my life, what do I need to say to God? (Here you can name feelings and thoughts that arose while reading the text.)

- What difference does this text make in my life? How am I going to respond to what just emerged in prayer? How am I willing to change?

Lectio divina is not about the "product" of this process but about being present and open to God. Scriptures are the living word of God: the Holy Spirit is working through them. Expect to be surprised by this prayer experience!

Another way to pray with Scripture is to memorize verses that strike you. Perhaps write them in a notebook, or mark them in your Bible so that you can easily refer to them later. Favorite passages from the prophets, from the psalms, from the Gospels (or any other book of the Bible) can become the structure around which you build your prayer life. Drawing on the riches of Scripture is important for developing and deepening your personal prayer.

In the chapters that follow, I've included selections of Scripture passages that seem to resonate with many believers or have become important for me. I hope that you'll add your own Bible verses and thus make this prayer book your own.

Praying with Visual Arts

"A picture is worth a thousand words" goes the saying. Indeed, images can connect with our emotions, can evoke a response from us, and can help us recognize and remember stories and truths.

It is not surprising, then, that since the days of the early Church, the visual arts have been an essential tool for expressing our faith. Jesus painted images with words in parables and metaphors for his listeners. Christians painted images based on Jesus' words and deeds. When we pray with visual arts, we find that word and image, revelation and interpretation, combine forces.

Visual arts are always an expression of a given culture. Praying with art from different eras and cultures can offer new appreciation for a story that has become too familiar. It can jar us out of our set patterns of thinking, allowing us to share in the insights that God granted to the artist.

I once had a particularly moving experience of the power of visual arts. Amid the usual hubbub of the international airport, a sign caught my eye: it advertised a temporary exhibition set up in one of the areas connecting the terminals. The Rijksmuseum had brought to the traveling public several paintings of the Old Dutch Masters, among other treasures. As I was standing in front of the paintings, I couldn't help but be touched by these masterpieces; the artists of old reached out and spoke to me from across the centuries.

I paused before Johannes Vermeer's *The Milkmaid*, an exquisite study in light and form, depicting a maid pouring milk as the light pours through the kitchen window. I know how painfully slowly Vermeer painted because he had to have every aspect of the picture just right: balance, composition, colors, light. I have a deep appreciation for the painting, partly because I know all of these things about the artist and partly for its sheer beauty, untouched by the passing of centuries.

I picked up a reproduction in the gift shop, and while the attendant wrapped it carefully, I said a prayer of thanks to God for soothing my aching soul with the beauty of the divine gift bestowed on this artist. I made my way to the gate, filled with the peace of God's presence, and boarded the plane to go to my mother's funeral.

Praying with Music

Come, let us sing joyfully to the L<small>ORD</small>;
    cry out to the rock of our salvation.
Let us come before him with a song of praise,
    joyfully sing out our psalms.

—P<small>SALM</small> 95:1-2

The power of music to help us connect to the transcendent, to the divine, is unsurpassable, for music engages our whole being, not just certain parts of our brains.

Why do we sing or chant certain parts of the Mass? Why are national anthems set to music? Why don't people just recite them? Because saying the words does not have the same effect on us as singing them together.

Singing, listening to music, or playing a musical instrument can help us develop our personal relationship with God.

Some chapters of this prayer book include text of hymns that you can pray by singing.

Be filled with the Spirit, addressing one another [in]
psalms and hymns and spiritual songs, singing and
playing to the Lord in your hearts, giving thanks always
and for everything in the name of our Lord Jesus Christ
to God the Father.

—Ephesians 5:18-20

Let the word of Christ dwell in you richly,
as in all wisdom you teach and admonish one another,
singing psalms, hymns, and spiritual songs with
gratitude in your hearts to God.

—Colossians 3:16

Shout with joy to the Lord, all the earth;
    break into song; sing praise.
Sing praise to the Lord with the lyre,
    with the lyre and melodious song.
With trumpets and the sound of the horn
    shout with joy to the King, the Lord.

—Psalm 98:4-6

Chapter Two

BEGINNINGS—SETTING OUT— PLANTING SEEDS

In the beginning was the Word,
  and the Word was with God,
  and the Word was God.
He was in the beginning with God.
  All things came to be through him,
  and without him nothing came to be.
What came to be through him was life,
  and this life was the light of the human race;
  the light shines in the darkness,
  and the darkness has not overcome it.

—JOHN 1:1-5

Beginnings in life can be exhilarating, anxiety provoking, hope-filled, and frustrating—or any combination thereof. It all depends, doesn't it? It depends on the circumstances under which this beginning happens. Life transitions of all

sorts, whether willingly chosen or not, or occurring as a matter of course, evoke a range of emotions that we can easily recall. Questions like "Remember the first . . . ?" or "Remember when . . . ?" may lead us on a roller-coaster ride of feelings, regardless of our willingness to engage our emotions. Sit for a few minutes and remember. Note the range of feelings these memories evoke, name them, and describe them.

Feelings and emotions are morally value neutral; that is, having a certain feeling is neither good nor wrong in and of itself. The psalms are a great example of giving expression to a wide range of thoughts and emotions: from beseeching God (Psalm 38:2) to demanding action from God (Psalm 26:1), from joyful thanksgiving (Psalm 66) to fear (Psalm 6:2), from lamenting one's situation (Psalm 13:2) to being angry (Psalm 58), and many others.

Starting out on this journey of prayer may also elicit some feelings. Whether you are curious, excited, a little unsure, or setting out confidently, what matters most is your willingness to try. However, recognizing what and how you feel when you pray will help deepen your self-understanding, your connection to God, and your connection to fellow human beings.

An important aspect of beginning any new endeavor is creating a space, both literally and figuratively, in which this new endeavor can take place. In other words, we develop certain routines that facilitate our engagement. When it comes to prayer, consider the following questions: Is there a designated time and place that you will set aside for prayer? What do you need to do to establish a routine that can support your prayer? For instance, if you get easily distracted, you will need a space that offers no or few distractions. If you would like to engage your whole body, you need enough room to do so; if you rely on music or the visual arts, you need to have access to them, and so on. Getting ready is part of beginnings.

This chapter includes prayers about different kinds of beginnings that we may notice in nature, beginnings we experience in human life, or beginnings that are part of our Catholic heritage.

—Be Light for Us, O Christ—

Be light for us, O Christ,
this short, short winter day,
that we may see to run by faith
amid the dark and gray.

Be light for us, O Christ,
this cold, cold winter day,
that we may feel your warmth and touch
with every healing ray.

Be light for us, O Christ,
this spare, spare winter day:
a light that brings a quiet peace
and gathers us to pray.

Be light for us, O Christ,
this good, good winter day,
that we may radiate your word
with every word we say.

Be light for us, O Christ,
this new, new winter day,
that with the dawn our praise may rise
and fill the coming day.

—HARRY HAGAN, OSB[1]

—New Beginnings—

O God of life,
who chooses creation over chaos
and new beginnings over emptiness,
we bring to you the disorder of our nations and world
and the emptiness of our lives and relationships.
Bless us and the nations with the grace of creativity.
Bless us and all people with the hope of new beginnings.

—J. PHILIP NEWELL[2]

17

—Morning Offering—

As a new day stirs, my prayer greets you:
let all whom I encounter catch a glimpse of your love;
let all that comes my way be a harbinger of your
    presence;
let all of me glorify you, most Holy Trinity!

—A Morning Prayer—

Grant us, O Lord, to pass this day in gladness and peace,
without stumbling and without stain; that reaching the even-
tide victorious over all temptation, we may praise you, the
eternal God, who is blessed and governs all things, world
without end.
Amen.

—Mozarabic Liturgy[3]

—*A New Day*—

Thank you, Lord, for the blessings of this day!
I may not know what the day will bring,
but I do know you are with me
as you have been through all my yesterdays.
Give me courage to meet the day's challenges,
grant me wisdom to handle them well,
and open my heart to love as you love.
May I be your blessing for others today!

—*Today Is a Gift*—

Today is a gift from God.
I can overlook it, or
    I can live it, love it, and leave the world better for it.
I can waste it, lamenting what I don't have, or
    I can seize its power to change my life.
I can ignore it, or
    I can embrace it to grow closer to God and those I love.

I can spend it bitter over yesterday, or
   I can spend it better—letting go and forgiving.
I can live in its shadows, or
   I can shed light, shine love, and share peace.
Whatever I decide, tomorrow is always determined by
   how I spent today.

—LISA O. ENGELHARDT[4]

—Sounds of Presence—

What a sound-soaked morning!
Birds compete with a lawn mower
making its way down the road.
Diesel motors cut through the serenity of cool breezes,
a break in the heat of summer.
Thank you for surrounding me!
Thank you for the gift of sound
that reminds me of your presence in creation:
You are near, you are here, you are.
Help me hear you in all your disguises today!

—Little Things—

God of hope, you reveal yourself in the little things
   of life.
Open our eyes and make us sensitive to your presence
   and action
in the ordinary places and events of life.
Amen.

—Duties of the Day—

The Lord walks among the pots and pans helping you
   both interiorly and exteriorly.

—St. Teresa of Ávila

—Flowers and Plants—

You've outdone yourself with the burst of colors
   and forms!
Praise and glory be for this beautiful diversity that is a
   perennial reminder of your limitless creativity!

—A Gaelic Blessing—
(Traditional)

Deep peace of the running wave to you,
Deep peace of the flowing air to you,
Deep peace of the quiet earth to you,
Deep peace of shining stars to you,
Deep peace of the Son of Peace to you.
Amen.

—Morning Prayer in Time of Stress—

Holy Spirit, fiery friend, guide me through this turmoil:
  ease the vise of stress,
lift the cloud of worry,
shine your light into my darkness,
that I may see you and praise you,
to find you anew!

—Prayer of St. Prisca—
(Traditional)

O Lord God, Eternal King! You who stretched out the heavens and built the earth. You who put limits on the ocean and trampled the Serpent's head. You, O Lord, do not abandon me now. Hear my prayer.

—Known by God—

Before I formed you in the womb I knew you,
  before you were born I dedicated you,
  a prophet to the nations I appointed you.

—JEREMIAH 1:5

23

—Confidence in the Future—

For I know well the plans I have in mind for you—oracle
of the Lord, plans for your welfare and not for woe, so
as to give you a future of hope.

—Jeremiah 29:11

—Prayer from Christmas Mass—

In the wonder of the Incarnation,
   your eternal Word has brought to the eyes of faith
   a new and radiant vision of your glory.
In [Christ] we see our God made visible
   and so are caught up in love of the God we cannot see.

—The Roman Missal[5]

—*Magnificat*—

My soul proclaims the greatness of the Lord;
  my spirit rejoices in God my savior.
For he has looked upon his handmaid's lowliness;
  behold, from now on will all ages call me blessed.
The Mighty One has done great things for me,
  and holy is his name.
His mercy is from age to age
  to those who fear him.
He has shown might with his arm,
  dispersed the arrogant of mind and heart.
He has thrown down the rulers from their thrones
  but lifted up the lowly.
The hungry he has filled with good things;
  the rich he has sent away empty.
He has helped Israel his servant,
  remembering his mercy,
according to his promise to our fathers,
  to Abraham and to his descendants forever.

—LUKE 1:46-55

25

—Visitation—

She hurried to greet her cousin,
blood and circumstance tethering them closer:
new life greeting new life,
signaling the in-breaking of the divine into humble,
    human existence.
May we greet one another as if we were Mary
    and Elizabeth,
recognizing in each other the spark of divine life
and embracing the audacity of being chosen to
    become mothers.

—Expectant Mother—

O, what a miracle a baby is! I stand in awe that you have
entrusted me, loving God, to share in your creative power.
Bless this new life growing within me; protect us from harm
so that in giving birth we may give you glory!

—Growing Family—

My heart speeds up, not quite able to keep pace with the rapid heartbeat heralding that our family is growing. Who will this child be, Lord? I hope and pray that she or he will be yours. Loaned to us for loving and caring, for growing and flourishing, may it be so, may it be!

—Facing Infertility—

Lord, grant me the ability to accept
that a child of my heart will not be a child of my womb.
Soothe this pain.
Lift my disappointment.
Give me courage to open my heart to a child
    who needs a mother.
Lead me in your ways so that, in turn,
I may lead a child to you!

—A Prayer for the Sorrowing—

Almighty God, Comforter of the sad, Strength of sufferers, let our troubled prayers come before you, so that we may rejoice to find that your mercy is present with us in our troubles; through Jesus Christ our Lord. Amen.

—Gelasian Sacramentary[6]

—Gratitude—

Surely, I wait for the Lord;
    who bends down to me and hears my cry,
Draws me up from the pit of destruction,
    out of the muddy clay,
Sets my feet upon rock,
    steadies my steps,
And puts a new song in my mouth,
    a hymn to our God.

—Psalm 40:2-4

—*Life in God*—

Sometimes it is all too much.
Don't know where you begin and where I end.
Perhaps that's how it supposed to be—
lost in you without losing me.

—*Enthusiasm*—

En-theo—God within.
No wonder that enthusiasm is contagious,
for who could resist your energy charging our souls?
En-theo—God within.
May I never be afraid of catching enthusiasm!

—Divine Dance—

Oh, divine dance, most Holy Trinity!
A perfect synchrony of give-and-take;
no false steps that make us stumble and lose the beat;
no stilted conversation,
just the joy of being one for the other,
three-in-one gliding smoothly,
one-two-three, one-two-three through eternity.
Shall we dance?

—Baptism—

You claimed me as your own:
bathed in water, signed with chrism, marked with
    the cross,
I am yours.
Washed and sealed, now I follow,
sometimes hesitantly, sometimes without reserve.
Help me remember that I am beloved.

Shore me up with the fragrance of salvation.
Let me rest in the crux of your love.
You claimed me—I am yours.

—*Today*—

My life is an instant, a fleeting hour.
My life is a moment, which swiftly escapes me.
O my God, you know that on earth
I have only today to love you.

—St. Thérèse of Lisieux

—*Trinity*—

You, o eternal Trinity, are a deep sea into which,
the more I enter, the more I find, the more I seek.
O abyss,
O eternal Godhead,
O sea profound,
What more could you give me than yourself? Amen.

—St. Catherine of Siena

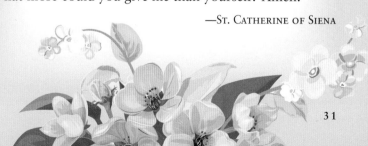

31

—The Spirit at Work—

Holy Spirit,
giving life to all life,
moving all creatures,
root of all things,
washing them clean,
wiping out their mistakes,
healing their wounds,
you are our true life,
luminous, wonderful,
awakening the heart
from its ancient sleep.

—HILDEGARD OF BINGEN

—Guidance—

You have been told, O mortal, what is good,
  and what the LORD requires of you:
Only to do justice and to love goodness,
  and to walk humbly with your God.

—MICAH 6:8

—First Day—

The backpack swallows up my child as she proudly heads for the door. It is the first day of kindergarten. She is ready. I am anxious. Will my baby be accepted? How will she handle the flood of new relationships, rules, and environment? Lord, you said: let the little children come to me. Here she is. I entrust my child to your care. Grant me your peace, especially today.

—Getting Ready—

Work and world await.
Grant me strength to meet each with confidence
that finds its source
in your unsurpassable love for me.

—Bookmark of St. Teresa of Ávila—

Let nothing disturb you,
nothing frighten you,
all things are passing;
God never changes.
Patience obtains all things:
one who God possesses wants nothing,
for God alone suffices.

—ST. TERESA OF ÁVILA

—Harvest Thanks and Petition—

May God be gracious to us and bless us;
  may his face shine upon us.

So shall your way be known upon the earth,
  your victory among all the nations.
May the peoples praise you, God;
  may all the peoples praise you!

May the nations be glad and rejoice;
  for you judge the peoples with fairness,
  you guide the nations upon the earth.

May the peoples praise you, God;
  may all the peoples praise you!

The earth has yielded its harvest;
  God, our God, blesses us.
May God bless us still;
  that the ends of the earth may revere him.

—Psalm 67:2-8

—*Friendship*—

Faithful friends are a sturdy shelter;
   whoever finds one finds a treasure.
Faithful friends are beyond price,
   no amount can balance their worth.
Faithful friends are life-saving medicine;
   those who fear God will find them.
Those who fear the Lord enjoy stable friendship,
   for as they are, so will their neighbors be.

—Sirach 6:14-17

—God of Beginnings—

O God of beginnings,
in earth's cycles and seasons, you offer us new life.
Bless this next season of life on our journey with you:
bless us with eyes to see new signs of promise,
bless us with ears to hear fresh, bold harmonies,
bless us with hands to reach for the unknown,
bless us with a mouth that proclaims your presence,
bless us with a heart beating with the joy of living!
Amen.

—God of Eternity—

God of eternity,
who has no beginning or end,
you found us, time-bound creatures, to be very good.
Grant that as this day unfolds, we awaken to moments
when time bursts open to the eternal and reveals
true beauty and goodness.

Chapter Three

BEARING FRUIT—STAYING THE COURSE—ESTABLISHING

Blessed are those who trust in the LORD;
    the LORD will be their trust.
They are like a tree planted beside the waters
    that stretches out its roots to the stream:
It does not fear heat when it comes,
    its leaves stay green;
In the year of drought it shows no distress,
    but still produces fruit.

—JEREMIAH 17:7-8

This is the season in which the broad contours of life are set, and we fill in the details. You might think of the period after a major life event that usually spans a longer stretch.

For instance, settling into young adult life, or marriage and family life beyond the first year, or establishing yourself in a career or profession.

This is a season of routines. We develop and maintain routines to help us navigate the daily demands of life. Yet routines can also get in the way of noticing and engaging new people, events, and circumstances through which God might reach out to us.

As to prayer, these are times when we have figured out and are comfortable with our prayer life. It can be a time of ever-deepening relationship with God or a time of just treading water, not wading into the deep. Wherever we might find ourselves, the good news is, there is more: more details to add and more colors to use as we fill in the details.

Another characteristic of this season is confidence: having achieved a certain level of expertise since we began, we now confidently take on what life has in store for us. We count on our strength—physical and inner alike—on our creativity, and on our can-do attitude to tackle problems successfully. In the process, we might forget who the source

39

of our strength and creativity is, to whom praise and thanksgiving belong. This is a season in the spiritual journey in which we need to be very intentional about cultivating an attitude of gratitude along with a can-do attitude.

This chapter includes prayers about daily life—the details that fill out the contours of our lives. These mundane events are proper subjects of prayer, for it is in and through them that we encounter the source of all our blessings, God.

—God's Welcome—

What no eye has seen, nor ear heard,
   nor the human heart conceived,
what God has prepared for those who love him.

—1 CORINTHIANS 2:9 (NRSV)

—*How to Be a Christian*—

Put on then, as God's chosen ones, holy and beloved, heartfelt compassion, kindness, humility, gentleness, and patience, bearing with one another and forgiving one another, if one has a grievance against another; as the Lord has forgiven you, so must you also do. And over all these put on love, that is, the bond of perfection. And let the peace of Christ control your hearts, the peace into which you were also called in one body. And be thankful. Let the word of Christ dwell in you richly, as in all wisdom you teach and admonish one another, singing psalms, hymns, and spiritual songs with gratitude in your hearts to God. And whatever you do, in word or in deed, do everything in the name of the Lord Jesus, giving thanks to God the Father through him.

—COLOSSIANS 3:12-17

41

—*The Suscipe of Catherine McAuley*—

My God, I am yours for time and eternity.
Teach me to cast myself entirely
into the arms of your loving Providence
with a lively, unlimited confidence in your
   compassionate, tender pity.
Grant, O most merciful Redeemer,
That whatever you ordain or permit may be acceptable
   to me.
Take from my heart all painful anxiety;
let nothing sadden me but sin,
nothing delight me but the hope of coming to the
   possession of you my God and my all, in your everlasting kingdom.
Amen.

—A Challenge by the Prophet—

But let justice roll down like waters,
  and righteousness like an ever-flowing stream.

—Amos 5:24 (NRSV)

—A Prayer in Times of Distress—

Lord, I am struggling.
I yearn for peace yet am mired in sorrow.
My heart is heavy;
hate and violence unfolded
to unveil a festering sickness
eating away our dignity as people, as a nation.
What am I to do? How do I respond?
Help me find a way; help me find your way,
for inaction and silence are burdens beyond pain.
Speak, Lord; your servant is listening!
Peace be with you!

Your words echo in my ears but find no resonance in
  my heart.
Peace eludes me.
Open my heart;
help me let go of what keeps me from your peace.
Burrow in, God of peace;
let your love push through these crusty walls and
  fill me to the brim
so darkness has no room and
  peace may reign again.

Creator God,
help us see your hand in the details of life.
Lead us to trust that even flaws and disappointments
  can bring blessings.
With the company of angels,
may we praise your name forever.
Amen.

—Allergies—

God of Delight,
I marvel at your creation—from a distance.
For when I am in its midst, it scratches my throat,
clouds my vision, and irritates my nasal passages.
Help my body delight in your creation
as my heart delights in you!

—Total Eclipse—

Sunshine lifts my spirit. The night calms my soul.
In the total eclipse—the moon blocking the sun—
radiance and darkness unite to show forth your glory!
I stand in awe, in thanksgiving and utter joy.

—Imagination—

What a gift you have given us,
what a necessary gift!
Without it we stand dumbfounded, clod-footed,
stuck in the world of our limited perceptions,
never reaching beyond our time-bound existence,
never able to follow our unceasing yearning for you.
Praise be to you, God of all,
for imagination that created and
continues to create visions of your glory!

—Support—

Come to me, all you who labor and are burdened, and I will
give you rest. Take my yoke upon you and learn from me,
for I am meek and humble of heart; and you will find rest
for yourselves. For my yoke is easy, and my burden light.

—MATTHEW 11:28-30

—Whirring Mind—

What comes first? How do I decide? Where is your guidance when I am most in need of it? My mind races around and around, unable to veer off its track, circling without effect other than making me feel overwhelmed and trapped. Help me find you at the center; let your presence slow and steady my thoughts, that I may see beyond the whirring images that obscure your plan.

—Traffic—

I sit behind the wheel, trying hard to practice the virtue of patience. It is a challenge of great proportions in this stop-and-go traffic. I know we all have places to be. It is poor city planning that keeps us inching along together for miles on end. I see the sullen look of the preteen boy who'd rather be almost anywhere, except for the lure of dinner at the end of the trip. I see the young mom whose

toddler behind her is ready to loose the restraints of the car seat. I see the elderly couple nervously checking signs for the right exit. Keep us safe, St. Christopher, patron of travelers. Watch out for us, all you guardian angels. May we all make it to our destination today!

—*Preparing a Meal*—

Mouths to feed,
hearts to heal,
friendships to forge:
cooking is God's work,
even if I am its executor,
skilled, willing, yet sometimes resentful.
Grant me largeness of spirit;
may my chopping, basting, and sautéing
bring you close to all who sit around the table.

—Enough—

Am I doing it right?

Is it holy enough that I am feeding, clothing, and
nurturing my child?

Come, Holy Spirit; fill my heart;

drive out the whispers of uncertainty that divert me
from my call as a parent.

Strengthen my resolve to live each day seeking your
guidance.

Let me lean on your gentle reminder:

It is enough. You are enough. I love you.

—*Expectations*—

Dear God,

You know I try to do my best as a parent.

There are so many good things I'd like to do with and for my family;

help me keep my priorities straight;

help me discern what are realistic expectations of myself and not be blinded by false messages about what I should be doing.

Help me leave aside doing things for the sake of appearance and focus on building up our relationships with you and with each other.

Grant me wisdom to measure by your standards, and give me strength to follow through.

Amen.

—Handing on Faith—

Loving and merciful God,
you have gifted us with faith
and called us to share our faith with others.
Give us the courage to bear witness
to your redeeming love in words and deeds.
Open our hearts and minds to your presence in the
    world,
especially in those we serve.
We ask this in the name of your beloved Son, Jesus, who
    lives and reigns with you and the Holy Spirit, one
    God, for ever and ever.
Amen.

51

—Prayer before a Meeting—

God of abundance,
you have fed your people with heavenly food in the
    desert;
and have given yourself as nourishment for our
    Christian journey;
look with favor upon our gathering;
help us to respond to the leaven of your Holy Spirit,
give us patience to allow the Spirit to work,
wisdom to know our limits, and
courage to be consumed in your service.
Grant this through our Lord, Jesus Christ, your Son,
who lives and reigns with you and the Holy Spirit,
one God, for ever and ever.
Amen.

—Prosper the Work of Our Hands—

Lord, prosper the work of our hands!
Creating, comforting, caressing,
holding, healing, helping,
giving, guiding, guarding—
may our hands do godly work, Lord;
prosper the work of our hands!

—In Times of Distraction—

Quiet my racing thoughts and heart, that I may focus on
the task at hand. Tame my imagination, gather my scat-
tering fancies, and channel their energy into work that is
pleasing to you!

—*Feeling Overwhelmed*—

There are so many things that need my attention; I am floundering in accomplishing anything! Come, Holy Spirit; guide me into the discipline of tackling one thing at a time. Help me to keep going until the true needs of the day are met.

—*College Bound*—

Loving God,
All those years ago, you have entrusted this child to our care. We nurtured and taught our child to follow you. As we prepare to take him to start college, help us to loosen our hold without ever breaking the bonds of love. Guide and protect our child, that he may hold fast to the values we have instilled and may flourish and grow into the person you envisioned.

I pray in the name of your beloved Son, our Lord Jesus Christ, who lives and reigns with you and the Holy Spirit, one God for ever and ever. Amen.

—*Being Grand*—

Bone of my bone and flesh of my flesh,
a child of my child—a grand child, a grandchild!
This tiny new life brings back memories of bygone days,
forces me to relearn forgotten skills
and develop new ones, if I am to keep up with him.
Grant me wisdom beyond my years,
energy that belies my years,
and a joyful spirit, so that our years together
may bond us beyond bone and flesh.
Amen.

—*Single*—

I wish people would stop making assumptions about my single status! I may not have chosen the single life, but I accept that that is your choice for me, God.

I want to live it according to your plans—so please help me deal with well-meaning but misguided people who cannot image its richness and judge it only in terms of their family life.

I am from a family, and I am family to others—some like me, some with families of their own. Help people recognize the dignity of the single life, and grant me joy that discredits their assumptions.
Amen.

—Love of God—

If the love you have for me
Is like the love I have for you,
My God, what detains me?
Oh, what is delaying you?

— St. Teresa of Ávila

—Breastplate—

Christ with me, Christ before me, Christ behind me,
Christ in me, Christ beneath me, Christ above me.
Christ on my right, Christ on my left,
Christ when I lie down, Christ when I sit down, Christ
    when I arise,
Christ in the heart of everyone who thinks of me,
Christ in the mouth of everyone who speaks of me,
Christ in every eye that sees me,
Christ in every ear that hears me.

—St. Patrick

—Service—

Christ has no body now but yours.

No hands, no feet on earth but yours.

Yours are the eyes through which he looks compassion on
   this world.

Yours are the feet with which he walks to do good.

Yours are the hands through which he blesses all the
   world.

Yours are the hands, yours are the feet, yours are the eyes,
   you are his body.

Christ has no body now on earth but yours.

Amen.

—St. Teresa of Ávila (attributed)

—Supplication—

Draw near, O Lord, our God; graciously hear us, guilty of
   sinning before you!
Attende Domine, et miserere, quia peccavimus tibi.

—Mozarabic hymn[7]

—Blessed Be Your Purity—

Blessed be your purity,
May it be blessed for ever,
For no less than God takes delight
In such exalted beauty.
To you, heavenly princess,
Holy Virgin Mary,
I offer on this day
My whole heart, life, and soul.
Look upon me with compassion;
Do not leave me, my mother.

—Traditional Latin American Prayer

—I Believe—

"I am with you always, until the end of the age."
I know you know my pain.
I know you see my tears.
I know you are with me.
So I dare feel the pain.
I dare shed tears.
I dare lean into my sorrow.
I believe you'll soothe my pain.
I believe you'll dry my tears.
I believe. I believe.

—Asking for Forgiveness—

It is so hard to ask for forgiveness;
to look into the eyes of another and say
what has weighed on me for some time,
to pry open the shell of self-protection,
to chance being hurt.
Again.
Let me tap into your courage, dear Jesus!
Inspire my words to flow with sincerity.
May they plant the seed of peace between us!
May it be.
Amen.

—Hymn of a Grateful Heart—

I thank you, Lord, with all my heart;
   in the presence of the angels to you I sing.
I bow low toward your holy temple;
   I praise your name for your mercy and faithfulness.
For you have exalted over all
   your name and your promise.
On the day I cried out, you answered;
   you strengthened my spirit.

—Psalm 138:1-3

—*Forgiveness*—

The words cut deeply, robbing me of breath,
    shaking me to the core.
Why would anybody do that?

I am dumbfounded yet resolute:
I will not let this twist what is beautiful
into an instrument of pain to be inflicted on others.
I will not succumb to my desire to lash out in hurt.

Dear Jesus, you know the sense and physical pain of
    betrayal.
Grant me what I still require to be able to journey
    toward forgiveness.
Amen.

Chapter Four

HARVESTING—SLOWING DOWN— CHANGING COURSE

There is an appointed time for everything,
and a time for every affair under the heavens.
A time to give birth, and a time to die;
a time to plant, and a time to uproot the plant.
A time to kill, and a time to heal;
a time to tear down, and a time to build.
A time to weep, and a time to laugh;
a time to mourn, and a time to dance.
A time to scatter stones, and a time to gather them;
a time to embrace, and a time to be far from embraces.
A time to seek, and a time to lose;
a time to keep, and a time to cast away.
A time to rend, and a time to sew;
a time to be silent, and a time to speak.
A time to love, and a time to hate;
a time of war, and a time of peace.

—ECCLESIASTES 3:1-8

There comes a time in life when inevitable changes force us to confront how we ourselves are changing. Looking into the metaphorical mirror is not easy, for we need to acknowledge our losses, to humbly name our contributions, to gather in the fruits of living and loving, to face transition as a necessary part of becoming who we were and are meant to be. All this takes courage, humility, and trust. As a result of this process, we might realize that we have to change course or, if on the right course, have to change speed, pulling back on the throttle.

In the spiritual life, this is a season of slowing down: of treasuring the moments of being rather than cramming them full of doing, of encountering God in change, amidst transitions, in silence. This is a time of practicing contemplation, of letting go of outside expectations, of trying out new ways to pray. This is a time for seeing with new eyes.

The prayers in this chapter reflect the transitional nature of this season, with the joys and struggles that accompany any transition.

—*Fall*—

Dear God, it feels like a fall morning in my little corner of the world. The air is clean and crisp. But fall has always been a hard season for me. It feels like a little piece of me dies as all the flowers fade, the leaves fall, and the trees go bare. Help me to look at fall differently this year. Help me make this a time to reflect on all that I have been given, a time to be grateful for all I have, and a time to prepare for a new season in your world and in my life.

—LINDA BIEKER[8]

—Changing—

It took me a long while
to see beyond my discomfort,
the lack of convenience,
to find you in the rolling hills,
cultivated fields, and winding roads.
City dweller adjusting to rural living.
Now I marvel at the dedication of farmers.
Slow-moving farm equipment is no longer
   a source of frustration
but a chance to catch my breath and be grateful
for those whose toil allows me to put pen to paper
   and fresh food on the table.

—In Due Time—

The bright green of spring turned to its deeper shades
    before heat and drought desiccated it to brown. My
    stomach tightens with each crunching step.
How long before rain comes?
How long before farmers' prayers are answered?
How long before wildlife need not brave the company
    of humans to find food?
How long?
I hear the psalmist giving voice to the Israelites'
    yearning, frustration—and trust.
Asking the question implies an answer,
even if it is—in due time.

—Finding Our Voice—

It took time to figure out who I am: to truly believe
    that I am made in your image and likeness, that I am
    beloved.
What would it be like if each one of us would believe
    and live the belief? Might it cut through our defensive-
    ness, mitigate our fears, and open us up wider to each
    other and to God?
Firmly rooted in our identity, finding our voice in Christ
    might be just what the world needs.
Let me speak words of consolation; let me be the spark
    of joy that fires love for you!

—*Listening*—

We are so used to noise that we filter it out with great
efficiency.
Today I am listening.
Listening to life around me:
birds chirping, vehicles passing,
the rustle of leaves on the breeze,
the occasional bark of dogs waking with the morning.
Everything speaks of you if only I listen.
"Open my ears, Lord"—
words and melody echo in my mind.
Open my ears, Lord, is my silent sigh.

—Discernment—

The phone rang.
An invitation came to consider changing course.
Which way do I go, Lord?
Grant me wisdom to discern this opportunity;
    may I not fall prey to my own vanity of being
    sought out;
may I be true to commitments already made without
   shying away from the possibility of growth that a new
   challenge implies.

—Senior Year—

"Do you realize that this is our last year together?"

The question stopped me in my tracks.

My child, to whom I just gave birth, has grown into a senior in high school. I know that we have been preparing her for venturing out, for forging her own path in life. Yet this moment snuck upon me and found me unprepared. Dear God, please help us make this transition mindfully. Open my heart to the guidance of your Holy Spirit. May I recognize ways through which I can best support her. Grant me courage to love this child of mine through the pain of separation, that she may emerge secure in our trust and set out confidently when the time comes.

May this be a year of grace in our relationship with you and with each other!
Amen.

—Pruning: A Meditation—

In our parish, the church building and the family life center are connected by a corridor that houses offices and also provides another entrance to the complex. Glass double doors, flanked by floor-to-ceiling windows, lead into the building. Another set, on the opposite side of the corridor, invites you to the meditation garden. During the winter months, the oversized potted ficus trees that stand as sentinels outside these doors are brought in to protect them from being damaged by the cold.

A few days before Christmas, as I stepped into the building, the sight of bare white branches greeted me, and I wondered fleetingly what had happened. Did some disease attack the trees, or were they exposed to the deep cold of the past days and suffer frostbite? It's a shame, I thought. I liked the leafy branches, even if they often created a bottleneck as people tried to negotiate around them in the hall. Now only a few green leaves remained at the tops of each. Later in the morning, I saw that someone was actually decorating the plants: it was not disease or frostbite,

73

but her vision that had altered their looks so drastically, eliciting comments from staff and volunteers.

Morning turned into afternoon. The decorator had been long gone when, passing by the trees, a stream of light hit me: the rays pouring through the glass panes bounced off the ornaments, throwing shadows on the carpet, enveloping gently these new creations in light. It took a radical pruning for me to be able to see the so-far hidden shape of the plants. What an appropriate metaphor for spiritual growth, I thought.

How often do we negotiate around our leafy branches filtering out light, the light of God! We take it for granted that they are there—all those habits and lack thereof—never even imagining the beauty of the bare branches, the core of who we are, of whose we are.

God of love and mercy, enable me to see my own overgrown leafy branches in need of pruning!

Grant me the strength of will to take out the shears, and guide my vision to shape them into an image pleasing to you. Amen.

—Lent—

As Lent approaches, my anxiety rises.
What do you ask of me this year? What will I have to give up? How can I stand losing one more loved one in this season of letting go? Grant me a new vision: may Lent be transformed from a time of grief and loss into a time of preparation for renewal, restoration, and resurrection! May it be, Lord. May it be!

—Music—

I think in terms of music; that is, a word or phrase
will bring to mind a song, a hymn, a melody.
And I sing—even when nobody can hear me,
when no sound leaves my throat.

I sing when I am happy; I sing when I'm in pain.
I sing because music is my sure path to you.
I sing—and weep trying to imagine your harmonies!

—Sometimes I Feel like a Motherless Child—

Sometimes I feel like a motherless child
a long way from home.
Sometimes I feel like I'm almost gone
way up in the heavenly land.

—African-American Spiritual

—Swing Low, Sweet Chariot—

Swing low, sweet chariot,
comin' for to carry me home;
Swing low, sweet chariot,
comin' for to carry me home.

—African-American Spiritual

—Peace Prayer—

Lord, make me an instrument of your peace:
where there is hatred, let me sow love;
where there is injury, pardon;
where there is doubt, faith;
where there is despair, hope;
where there is darkness, light;
where there is sadness, joy.

O divine Master, grant that I may not so much seek
to be consoled as to console,
to be understood as to understand,
to be loved as to love.
For it is in giving that we receive,
it is in pardoning that we are pardoned,
and it is in dying that we are born to eternal life.
Amen.

—St. Francis of Assisi

—*Surrender*—

Father, if you are willing, take this cup away from me;
   still, not my will but yours be done.

—LUKE 22:42

—*Peace*—

Peace, blessed peace!
A gift, a wish, a blessing;
a hard-won state of being
centered in Christ;
a response to the divine offer
that demands all of me.
Peace, blessed peace.

—Aches and Pains of Aging—

I am alive.
I feel my body—that is proof positive that I am alive.
The vigor of youth is oblivious to the body as a unity
   of different parts, for youth knows not that the role of
   joints later in life is to make known, without a doubt,
   that we exist.
I feel my body.
I am alive.
Thanks be to God!

—Losing Flexibility—

Joints creak, muscles strain, limbs get heavier with age.
What once was child's play
now demands warming up and stretching,
carefully tuning into movements,
lest they backfire and freeze me in place.

Grant me, gracious God, a nimble mind
to balance my body's loss of flexibility.

—Playfulness—

I need to lighten up; where has my playfulness gone? Why is it so hard to relax and enjoy what life is offering, especially through other people? Break through my crusty heart! Invigorate my tired self! Open me up to the joy of play, so that in play, I can find you again!

—Curiosity—

Lord, grant me the gift of curiosity, that I may never tire of learning, I may delight in exploring, and remain open to your surprises!

—Discovery: A Meditation—

Etched into my memory are moments of profound joy and excitement that come from discovery: the eureka moments of life that have the power to alter what comes after—as if the Holy Spirit is breaking in with scintillating precision and cutting through the veil of human limitation, for the moment.

The power manifested in that brilliance finds resonance in the cells of our bodies, and we are forever changed. With the passing of time, the facts might fade; but the visceral reaction, the feelings that the discovery evoked, remain and are brought to life, strengthened with each new meeting with the divine. Discovery unveils the divine, momentarily, partially—but profoundly.

Come, Holy Spirit; stir in us a sense of adventure; ignite our imagination; fuel our desire to seek you, meet you, and respond to you!

—Failing—

When I am insecure and afraid of trying,
help me remember, Lord,
that my biggest failings are not what didn't turn out as
    it ought to
but what I have failed to do: sins of omission.
Failed to grow in love,
failed to notice need,
failed to stand for truth and justice,
failed to bridge divides,
failed to follow you, Christ.
In your mercy, till my heart, open my eyes,
and stiffen my spine,
that I may be worthy of the name Christian.

—Stewardship—

Much will be required of the person entrusted with much, and still more will be demanded of the person entrusted with more (Luke 12:48).

Time, talent, treasure—all are a gift from you, gracious God.
I offer in your service all that you have entrusted to me.
Grant that I may be a faithful steward of these gifts.
May they contribute to your reign!

—I Have Been Blessed—

I have been blessed.
I have been blessed with family who love me.
I have been blessed with friends who support me.
I have been blessed with work that sustains me.
I have been blessed with play that delights me.
I have been blessed with faith that directs me.
I have been blessed. I am blessed.
I bless your name forever, my God!

—Epiphany and Epiphanies—A Reflection—

One of my favorite Christmas movies is *The Nativity Story* (2006), and some of my favorite scenes are of the three Wise Men, or Magi. We encounter them first in their observatory in Persia where they intently study the alignment of the stars and realize that something extraordinary is about to happen. Each of them represents a different and all too human response to that extraordinary sign: one is eager to take the perilous trip, another is reluctant to leave behind the comforts of home, and the third is just not interested in setting out on a fool's errand.

Ultimately, they do travel for months on end, find the newborn, and pay homage to God made manifest in the flesh.

• What is your nativity story, actual or spiritual?

• Who were the wise men and women in your life who showed up, out of nowhere, and brought gifts with them?

• How is God made manifest, that is, revealed in your life?

Chapter Five

STORING—RESTING—CONSERVING

Be still and know that I am God!

—PSALM 46:11

When our energy supplies are low, our body naturally enters conservation mode. It slows down, stores—sometimes in unwanted places—whatever energy is available. We find ourselves craving rest, and on occasion we wish we could hibernate like bears and their ilk. Low energy affects our outlook: we turn inward. Reminiscing about times gone by is suddenly our favorite activity.

Physical, psychological, emotional, and spiritual trauma can also lead to energy conservation: there are only so many inner resources available. All of it is needed to deal with the aftermath of trauma and to start the healing process. An essential part of the process is letting go in order to make room for healing to take place.

Whether we find ourselves in this season as a natural occurrence or as a response to some kind of trauma, its focus is putting things right and in order, and preparing to experience rebirth as we approach a new beginning in the cycle of life.

In our prayer life, this might be a season of quiet contemplation, reflection, gentle exploration, and making small but deliberate movements toward our ultimate goal of being with God.

Particularly suitable prayer forms are those involving the visual arts and music; both have the capacity to draw us into a new realm where we can encounter God.

—Call and Response—

You summoned and I answered; here I am.
You challenged and I struggled to discern your will.
You blessed and I am thankful.
Help me never to forget that you are the source of all
blessings.
Grant me wisdom to find my way to you.
Let me respond with Ignatius of Loyola:
your love and your grace are enough for me.

—Suscipe: Self-Offering—

Take, Lord, and receive all my liberty,
my memory, my understanding,
and my entire will,
All I have and call my own.
You have given all to me.

To you, Lord, I return it.
Everything is yours; do with it what you will.
Give me only your love and your grace,
that is enough for me.

—St. Ignatius of Loyola

—Images—

I often wonder about our images of you, Triune God.
Reflected in art throughout the ages,
    you wear a million disguises.
Sometimes we forget that what we depict is just a
    reflection,
a single-colored glass of a mosaic composed with infinite
    pieces.
Yet we need the tangible expressions
    that can lead us into your mystery.
Help us know the difference between what we see
    and who you are!

—A Study—

He stands, almost defiant, in half profile:
a bearded figure with shoulder-length dark hair,
in a torn white garment.
Head held high, looking right at his accuser.
This is a proud man or perhaps a just one
who knows who he is, and what this farce is all about.
Jesus before Pilate;
the painter before his peers;
a gift to my parents who now stand in God's presence . . .
Here I pray before history unfolding,
meaning layered into meaning.
The rest of the canvas recedes as I wonder:
would my voice be one among the many calling for your
    crucifixion?
Would I dare stand out in a mob whipped to frenzy by
    the spectacle?
Or would I stay home, out of sight, fretting and
    worrying about the happenings?

I don't know how I would respond.
But today, as I contemplate your image,
I am inspired to stand tall in the face of adversity.
I am emboldened to lean on you,
and so, I cling to you,
my Hungarian Jesus before Pilate,
my Lord Jesus, the Christ!

—Icon—

A prayer made visible.
A soul reaching out to you
in transcendent conversation that needs no words,
only an open, loving gaze.
A sense of order and tradition, handed down,
yet alive only in focused, studied, spirit-filled practicing.
A way of being and understanding
your presence in the world;
your presence to us, in and through images.
Sign, symbol, sacrament.
May my gaze find you gazing at me!

—To See with God's Eyes—

What do you see when you look at me?
A glance—and you know me like no other, including
    myself.
What do you see?

Do you see my doubts and fears?
Do you see what brings me joy?
Do you see a person desperately trying to . . . (you fill in
    the blank)?

Help me see beyond fear and doubt.
Help me treasure moments of joy.
Help me become the best version of the person you see.

Grant me sight that sees possibilities.
Grant me strength to sow joy.
Grant me wisdom to see with your eyes, my God!

*—Our Lady of Częstochowa
(The Black Madonna)—*

Our Lady of Częstochowa, you have inspired and protected countless people through the centuries to hold fast in times of trouble and to find their way to your Son, seated on your lap. Stained by soot, marked by arrows, erased and redrawn, you sit, wait, and guide our gaze: lead me to the Way, the Truth, to Life!

—Persistence—

When I hit the wall,
when I am spent and can't go on,
grant me the courage of the Samaritan woman
who would not let Jesus dismiss her without a hearing,
the persistence of Jeremiah
who could not keep silent about you,
and the whispers of your Holy Spirit to spur me on.
Amen.

—*Prayer of Confidence*—

All shall be well,
and all shall be well,
and all manner of thing shall be well.

—Julian of Norwich

—*Growing Older*—

As years rush by, the storehouse of memories fill steadily.
Remembering overtakes making new memories.
Lord, it is a hard task to keep up with who we were,
  where we trod, and what we contributed
  to your vision for our world.
May there always be memory keepers who hand down
  the stories of your people.
May we count among your people now and
when you gather us all in!

—Slowing Down—

The ordinary tasks of life take me longer these days. I do not mind. A life lived forever rushing is now settled into quiet, slow movements made more deliberate by actually pondering what I am doing. I like to think of it as mindful living. Thank you, God, for letting me reach this stage: unable to outrun you, now we can shuffle along together.

—Gratitude—

Thank you, Lord Jesus Christ,
For all the benefits and blessings
which you have given me,
for the pains and insults
which you have born for me.
Merciful Friend, Brother and Redeemer,
may I know you more clearly,
love you more dearly,
and follow you more closely,
day by day.

—St. Richard Chichester

—Prayer for Deliverance—

From cowardice that dare not face new truth,
from laziness that is contented with half-truth,
from the arrogance that thinks it knows all truth,
good Lord, deliver me.

—TRADITIONAL PRAYER FROM KENYA

—Sacred Heart—

O Heart of Love,
I put all my trust in you.
For I fear all things from my own weakness,
but I hope for all things from your goodness.

—ST. MARGARET MARY ALACOQUE

—Confidence in God—

Go forth in peace, for you have followed the good road.
Go forth without fear, for the one who created you has
made you holy, has always protected you, and loves you as
a mother. Blessed be you, my God, for having created me.

—St. Clare of Assisi

—Protection—

Blessed Lady, our mother,
Our great patroness of old,
In great need our country cries out to you:

Do not forget about our sweet homeland, Hungary,
and Hungarians who are in dire need.

—Traditional Hungarian Hymn

—Serenity—

God grant me
the serenity to accept the things are cannot change,
the courage to change the things I can,
and the wisdom to distinguish the one from the other.

—REINHOLD NIEBUHR

—Tears and Smiles—

One eye is laughing, the other is crying. It is the nature of saying goodbye as loved ones set out on a new journey. Even as I wish them well, the sting of separation remains. Be with me, Lord, so my tears might dry and my smiles might grow broader. Amen.

—Hope—

A bare tree amidst the faded green of late summer—
I recognize you.
Standing, still deeply rooted, hanging on to life;
not enough energy to sustain your leafy outer garment,
withered, yet waiting, ready for a new start.
Sentinel of gloaming—
I hope with you.

—Making Ends Meet—

Will it stretch far enough?
Once you fed five thousand
with just a few fish and loaves of bread.
Bless our meager provisions.
Stretch them enough to blunt the need
even if the ends won't meet.
I trust that you will provide.
Help me stay alert and follow your guiding hand.

—His Eye Is on the Sparrow—

Why should I feel discouraged, why should the shadows
   come,
why should my heart be lonely, and long for heav'n and
   home,
when Jesus is my portion? My constant friend is he:
His eye is on the sparrow, and I know he watches me;
His eye is on the sparrow, and I know he watches me.

Refrain:
I sing because I'm happy, I sing because I'm free,
For his eye is on the sparrow, and I know he watches me.

"Let not your heart be troubled," his tender word I hear,
and resting on his goodness, I lose my doubts and fears;
though by the path he leadeth, but one step I may see;
his eye is on the sparrow, and I know he watches me;
his eye is on the sparrow, and I know he watches me.
Whenever I am tempted, whenever clouds arise,

when songs give place to sighing, when hope within me
   dies,
I draw the closer to him, from care he sets me free;
his eye is on the sparrow, and I know he watches me;
his eye is on the sparrow, and I know he watches me.

—Civilla D. Martin

—For the Right Use of God's Gifts—

O Lord, our God, without whose will and pleasure not a
sparrow can fall to the ground,
grant to us in times of trouble to be patient without murmur-
ing or despair, and in prosperity to acknowledge your gifts,
and to confess that all our endowments come from you, O
Father of lights, who gives liberally and upbraids not. Give
us, by your Holy Spirit, a willing heart and a ready hand
to use all your gifts to your praise and glory; through Jesus
Christ our Lord. Amen.

—Archbishop Cranmer

—Evening Prayer—

Relieve and comfort, O Lord,
all the persecuted and afflicted;
speak peace to troubled consciences;
strengthen the weak;
confirm the strong;
instruct the ignorant;
deliver the oppressed;
and relieve the needy;
bring us all to the kingdom of rest and glory,
through Jesus Christ our Lord. Amen.

—ADAPTED FROM A PRAYER FROM 1613

—Evening Thanksgiving—

Accept our evening thanksgiving, O Fountain of all good,
who has led us in safety through the length of day;
who daily blessed us with so many mercies,
and has given us the hope of resurrection to eternal life;
through Jesus Christ our Lord. Amen.

—ANCIENT COLLECT

—Nunc Dimittis—Canticle of Simeon—

Now, Master, you may let your servant go
   in peace, according to your word,
for my eyes have seen your salvation,
   which you prepared in sight of all the peoples,
a light for revelation to the Gentiles,
   and glory for your people Israel.

—LUKE 2:29-32

—Precious Lord—

Precious Lord, take my hand.
Lead me on. Let me stand.
I am tired. I am weak. I am worn.
Through the storm,
through the night,
lead me on to the light.
Take my hand, precious Lord,
lead me home.

—AFRICAN-AMERICAN SPIRITUAL

PART TWO

~

A Rich Tradition of Prayer

Chapter Six

BASIC PRAYERS

—Sign of the Cross—

In the name of the Father, and of the Son, and of the
Holy Spirit.
Amen.

—The Glory Be (Doxology)—

Glory be to the Father, the Son, and the Holy Spirit;
as it was in the beginning, is now, and ever shall be
world without end.
Amen.

—The Lord's Prayer—

Our Father, who art in heaven,
hallowed be thy name.
Thy kingdom come.
Thy will be done on earth, as it is in heaven.
Give us this day our daily bread,
and forgive us our trespasses,
as we forgive those who trespass against us,
and lead us not into temptation,
but deliver us from evil.
Amen.

—The Hail Mary—

Hail Mary, full of grace, the Lord is with you;
blessed are you among women,
and blessed is the fruit of your womb, Jesus.
Holy Mary, Mother of God,
pray for us sinners
now and at the hour of our death.
Amen.

—Prayer to the Holy Spirit—

Come Holy Spirit, fill the hearts of your faithful
and kindle in them the fire of your love.
Send forth your Spirit and they shall be created,
And you shall renew the face of the earth.

—Act of Contrition—

My God,
I am sorry for my sins with all my heart.
In choosing to do wrong
and failing to do good,
I have sinned against you
whom I should love above all things.
I firmly intend, with your help,
to do penance,
to sin no more,
and to avoid whatever leads me to sin.
Our Savior Jesus Christ
suffered and died for us.
In his name, my God, have mercy.

—Act of Faith—

O my God, I firmly believe
that you are one God in three divine Persons,
Father, Son, and Holy Spirit.
I believe that your divine Son became man
and died for our sins and that he will come
to judge the living and the dead.
I believe these and all the truths
which the Holy Catholic Church teaches
because you have revealed them
who are eternal truth and wisdom,
who can neither deceive nor be deceived.
In this faith I intend to live and die.
Amen.

—*Act of Hope*—

O Lord God,
I hope by your grace for the pardon of all my sins
and after life here to gain eternal happiness
because you have promised it
who are infinitely powerful, faithful, kind, and merciful.
In this hope I intend to live and die. Amen.

—*Act of Love*—

O Lord God, I love you above all things
and I love my neighbor for your sake
because you are the highest, infinite and perfect
good, worthy of all my love.
In this love I intend to live and die.
Amen.

—*Guardian Angel Prayer*—

Angel of God, my Guardian dear,
to whom God's love commits me here,
ever this day be at my side
to light and guard, to rule and guide.
Amen.

—*Prayer to St. Michael the Archangel*—

Saint Michael Archangel,
defend us in battle,
be our protection against the wickedness and snares of
   the devil;
may God rebuke him, we humbly pray;
and do thou, O prince of the heavenly host,
by the power of God, cast into hell
Satan and all the evil spirits
who prowl through the world seeking the ruin of souls.
Amen.

—POPE LEO XIII

—Blessing before Meals—

Bless us, O Lord, and these your gifts,
which we are about to receive from your bounty,
through Christ, our Lord.
Amen.

—Grace after Meals—

We give you thanks, O Lord, for these your gifts,
which we have received from your goodness,
through Christ, our Lord. Amen.

Chapter Seven

MARIAN PRAYERS

—*Prayer to Our Lady of Guadalupe*—

Our Lady of Guadalupe, my mother,
into your hands joined in prayer,
take my prayers,
petitions, and hopes,
and present them to Jesus for me.
Remembering the love
and care your hands rendered to him,
he will not refuse what they hold now,
even though they are from me.
Amen.

—*Our Lady Help of Christians*—

Most holy virgin Mary, help of Christians,
how sweet it is to come to your feet
imploring your perpetual help.
If earthly mothers cease not to remember their children,
how can you, the most loving of all mothers, forget me?
Grant then to me, I implore you,
your perpetual help in all my necessities,
in every sorrow, and especially in all my temptations.
I ask for your unceasing help for all who are now
    suffering.
Help the weak, cure the sick, convert sinners.
Grant through your intercession many vocations to the
    religious life.
Obtain for us, O Mary, help of Christians,
that having invoked you on earth we may love and
    eternally thank you in heaven.

—St. John Bosco

—As a Little Child I Loved You—

As a little child,
I loved you like a mother.
Now that I am old,
my love for you has grown.
Receive me in heaven
as one of the blessed,
and I will proclaim
that I have obtained
such a great prize
through your patronage.
Amen.

—Pope Leo XIII[9]

—*Entrustment to Mary*—

Mother of the Redeemer,
with great joy we call you blessed.

In order to carry out his plan of salvation,
God the Father chose you before the creation
  of the world.
You believed in his love and obeyed his word.

The Son of God desired you for his mother
when he became man to save the human race.
You received him with ready obedience and
  undivided heart.

The Holy Spirit loved you as his mystical spouse
and filled you with singular gifts.
You allowed yourself to be led
by his hidden powerful action.

On the eve of the third Christian millennium,
we entrust to you the Church
which acknowledges you and invokes you as mother.

To you, mother of the human family and of the nations,
we confidently entrust the whole humanity,
with its hopes and fears.
Do not let it lack the light of true wisdom.
Guide its steps in the ways of peace.
Enable all to meet Christ,
the Way, the Truth, and the Life.

Sustain us, O Virgin Mary, on our journey of faith
and obtain for us the grace of eternal salvation.
O clement, O loving, O sweet mother of God
and our mother, Mary!

—Pope St. John Paul II[10]

—Mother of the Living Gospel—

Mary, Virgin and Mother,
you who, moved by the Holy Spirit,
welcomed the word of life
in the depths of your humble faith:
as you gave yourself completely to the Eternal One,
help us to say our own "yes"
to the urgent call, as pressing as ever,
to proclaim the good news of Jesus.

Filled with Christ's presence,
you brought joy to John the Baptist,
making him exult in the womb of his mother.
Brimming over with joy,
you sang of the great things done by God.
Standing at the foot of the cross
with unyielding faith,
you received the joyful comfort of the resurrection,
and joined the disciples in awaiting the Spirit

so that the evangelizing Church might be born.

Obtain for us now a new ardor born of the resurrection,
that we may bring to all the Gospel of life
which triumphs over death.
Give us a holy courage to seek new paths,
that the gift of unfading beauty
may reach every man and woman.

Virgin of listening and contemplation,
Mother of love, Bride of the eternal wedding feast,
pray for the Church, whose pure icon you are,
that she may never be closed in on herself
or lose her passion for establishing God's kingdom.

Star of the new evangelization,
help us to bear radiant witness to communion,
service, ardent and generous faith,
justice and love of the poor,
that the joy of the Gospel
may reach to the ends of the earth,

illuminating even the fringes of our world.

Mother of the living Gospel,
wellspring of happiness for God's little ones,
pray for us. Amen. Alleluia!

—POPE FRANCIS[11]

—Prayer of Love for Mary—

Holy Immaculate Mary, help all who are in trouble. Give courage to the fainthearted, console the sad, heal the infirm, pray for the people, intercede for the clergy, have a special care for nuns; may all feel, all enjoy your kind and powerful assistance, all who now and always render and will render you honor, and will offer you their petitions. Hear all our prayers, O Mother, and grant them all. We are all your children. Grant the prayers of your children. Amen forever.

—POPE ST. JOHN XXIII[12]

Chapter Eight

PRAYERS THROUGHOUT THE YEAR

—Advent Prayer—

Lord Jesus, master of both the light and the darkness,
send your Holy Spirit upon our preparations for Christmas.

We who have so much to do seek quiet spaces to hear
   your voice each day.
We who are anxious over many things look forward to
   your coming among us.
We who are blessed in so many ways long for the
   complete joy of your kingdom.
We whose hearts are heavy seek the joy of your presence.
We are your people, walking in darkness, yet seeking the
   light.
To you we say, "Come, Lord Jesus!"

—HENRI J. M. NOUWEN[13]

Prayers for Lighting the Advent Wreath Candles

First Week
Hope

Son of God, Emmanuel, you are our hope. As we enter Advent, help us to listen to your voice amidst the noise of our lives. May our preparations to celebrate your birth strengthen us in faith as we wait for your coming in glory at the end of times. Amen.

Second Week
Peace

Son of God, Prince of Peace, we yearn for you. In a world torn by violence and strife, we seek your gift of deep and abiding peace. Fill us with your presence, that we may share your peace with all whom we encounter. Amen.

Third Week
Joy

Son of God, joy of every heart, make your home in us. In lives marred by sadness and sorrow, may we find you anew. May our hearts expand in gratitude, for your coming makes our joy complete. Amen.

Fourth Week
Love

Son of God, Love Incarnate, gather us close. In the darkness and cold of winter, guided by your light and embraced by your love, may we help dispel darkness around us and bring your love to warm our corner of the world. Amen.

—AGNES KOVACS

—Advent Hymn
O Come, O Come, Emmanuel
(Catholic Version)—

O come, O come, Emmanuel,
And ransom captive Israel,
That mourns in lonely exile here,
Until the Son of God appear.
Rejoice! Rejoice! Emmanuel
Shall come to thee, O Israel.

O come, thou Wisdom from on high,
Who ord'rest all things mightily;
To us the path of knowledge show,
And cause us in her ways to go.
Rejoice! Rejoice! Emmanuel
Shall come to thee, O Israel.

O come, O come, thou Lord of might,
Who to thy tribes, on Sinai's height,
In ancient times didst give the law
In cloud and majesty and awe.
Rejoice! Rejoice! Emmanuel
Shall come to thee, O Israel.

O come, thou Rod of Jesse's stem
From every foe deliver them
That trust thy mighty pow'r to save,
And give them victory o'er the grave.
Rejoice! Rejoice! Emmanuel
Shall come to thee, O Israel.

O come, thou Key of David, come
And open wide our heav'nly home;
Make safe the way that leads on high,
And close the path to misery.
Rejoice! Rejoice! Emmanuel
Shall come to thee, O Israel.
O come, thou Dayspring, from on high,

124

And cheer us by thy drawing nigh;
Disperse the gloomy clouds of night,
And death's dark shadows put to flight.
Rejoice! Rejoice! Emmanuel
Shall come to thee, O Israel.

O come, Desire of nations, bind
in one the hearts of all mankind;
Bid thou our sad divisions cease;
And be thyself our Prince of Peace.
Rejoice! Rejoice! Emmanuel
Shall come to thee, O Israel.

—God Waits . . . We Wait—An Advent Prayer—

As the infant Christ waits in Mary's womb for birth,
so God waits to be birthed in human hearts,
midwifed through companion care.
As the aging Zechariah waits in quiet expectation,
God waits to be spoken,
uttered through servanthood.

As the trusting Magi wait for a sign,
God waits to be seen,
imaged in complexity.

"We wait in joyful hope,"
ah, perhaps, but often we wait
in impatient longing:
our vulnerable spirits ache for certainty;
our tender hearts yearn for truth;
our weary minds search for answers.

And we forget
that God waits
in impatient longing, too,
for the vulnerable to be sheltered,
the brokenhearted to find care,
the lost to be welcomed in love.
This is an Advent prayer, then.

May God's waiting and ours
find rest in each other's arms,
and may God's waiting come to completion
through our faithful, tender, strong, and merciful
imitation of the Christ who is, who was, and who is to come.

Amen, so be it.

—Author Unknown

—Advent at Midlife—

I am no longer waiting for a special occasion;
I burn the best candle on ordinary days.

I am no longer waiting for the house to be clean;
I fill it with people who understand that even dust
    is sacred.
I am no longer waiting for everyone to understand me;
it's just not their task.

I am no longer waiting for the perfect children;
my children have their own names that burn brightly as
    any star.

I am no longer waiting for the other shoe to drop;
it already did, and I survived.

I am no longer waiting for the time to be right;
the right time is always now.

128

I am no longer waiting for the mate who will
   complete me;
I am grateful to be warmly and tenderly held.

I am no longer waiting for a quiet moment;
my heart can be stilled whenever it is called.

I am no longer waiting for the world to be at peace;
I unclench my grasp and breathe peace in and out.

I am no longer waiting to do something great;
being awake to carry my grain of sand is enough.

I am no longer waiting to be recognized;
I know that I dance in a holy circle.

I am no longer waiting for forgiveness.
I believe, I believe.

—MARY ANNE PERRONE

—Rejoice—

Remember that you are beloved by God;
Embrace your life and keep
Jesus at the center;
Open yourself to experiences,
Invite others as God is inviting you;
Celebrate well and often, for
Emmanuel, God-With-Us!

—AGNES KOVACS

—I Am There (Christmas)—

Now God says to us
What he has already said to the earth as a whole
Through his grace-filled birth:

I am there. I am with you.
I am your life. I am your time.

I am the gloom of your daily routine. Why will you not hear it?

I weep your tears—pour yours out to me.

I am your joy.

Do not be afraid to be happy; ever since I wept, joy is the standard of living

That is really more suitable than the anxiety and grief of those who have no hope.

I am the blind alley of all your paths,

For when you no longer know how to go any farther,

Then you have reached me,

Though you are not aware of it.

I am in your anxiety, for I have shared it.

I am in the prison of your finiteness,

For my love has made me your prisoner.

I am in your death,

For today I began to die with you, because I was born,

And I have not let myself be spared any real part of this
experience.

I am present in your needs;

I have suffered them and they are now transformed.

I am there.

I no longer go away from this world.

Even if you do not see me now, I am there.

My love is unconquerable.

I am there.

It is Christmas.

Light the candles! They have more right to exist than all
the darkness.

It is Christmas.

Christmas that lasts forever.

—KARL RAHNER, S.J.[14]

In This Holy Season

Lord, in this holy season of prayer and song and laughter, we praise you for the great wonders you have sent us: for shining star and angel's song, for infant's cry in lowly manger. We praise you for the Word made flesh in a little Child. We behold his glory and are bathed in its radiance.

Be with us as we sing the ironies of Christmas, the incomprehensible comprehended, the poetry made hard fact, the helpless Babe who cracks the world asunder. We kneel before you, shepherds, innkeepers, wise men. Help us to rise bigger than we are. Amen.

—Author Unknown

Christmas Prayer

Blessed be the Lord God, who comes in the name of the Lord, and has dawned upon us;
whose coming has redeemed us, whose nativity
   enlightened us;

133

who by his coming has sought out the lost, and illuminated those who sat in darkness.

Grant, therefore, O Father Almighty, that we, celebrating with pious devotion the day of his nativity, may find the day of judgement a day of mercy; that as we have known his benignity as our Redeemer, we may feel his gentle tenderness as our Judge.

—Mozarabic Missal[15]

The Holy Family Prayer

Jesus, Son of God and Son of Mary, bless our family. Graciously inspire in us the unity, peace, and mutual love that you found in your own family in the little town of Nazareth.

Mary, Mother of Jesus and our mother, nourish our family with your faith and your love. Keep us close to your Son, Jesus, in all our sorrows and joys.

Joseph, foster-father to Jesus, guardian and spouse of Mary, keep our family safe from harm. Help us in all times of discouragement or anxiety.

Holy Family of Nazareth, make our family one with you. Help us to be instruments of peace. Grant that love, strengthened by grace, may prove mightier than all the weaknesses and trials through which our families sometimes pass. May we always have God at the center of our hearts and homes until we are all one family, happy and at peace in our true home with you. Amen.

—MISSIONARIES OF THE HOLY FAMILY[16]

A Lenten Prayer

O God, beneath whose eyes every heart trembles, and all consciences are afraid, be merciful to the groanings of all, and heal the wounds of all; that as not one of us is free from fault, so not one may be shut out from pardon. Through Jesus Christ our Lord.

—GELASIAN SACRAMENTARY[17]

—Stations of the Cross through Mary's Eyes—

Join Mary for a reflection as she guides us through the Stations of the Cross as seen through her eyes.

The First Station: Jesus Is Condemned to Die

My Son is standing there, facing his accusers with the calm of one who has completely surrendered to the will of God. I never thought that my "let it be" would lead here. I am praying for a miracle: for someone to defend him, for this Roman prefect to show some mercy . . . Can't he see that Jesus is innocent? Can't he see through the machinations of the religious leaders? How can a man without guilt be condemned to die?

Reflect on each station of his journey. Let us ask for God's grace to help us more fully enter the journey and grow in gratitude for its gift.

The Second Station: Jesus Carries His Cross

My beloved Son, who is used to carrying heavy wood, now shoulders this instrument of torture. Each step he takes cuts deeply into his already battered shoulders. I can't believe he could manage even a few steps. The crowd is growing as I follow from a distance through the streets, holding onto the arm of the younger Mary; among the gawkers and curiosity seekers, I recognize some of his followers. A few weeks ago, they sat at his feet listening. Now they cover their faces in fear.

Jesus takes up the weight of all of our crosses, all of our senseless suffering, and the weight of all sin in the world—past, present and future. Remember that this is for all of us. Each of us can say it was "for me." As we imagine each step he takes, we can pause now to say "Thank you," in our own words, deep in our hearts.

The Third Station: Jesus Falls the First Time

He falls. I want to scream "Stop this," but only a deep, ragged breath leaves my mouth as my heart breaks and I sink to the ground. How many times did I cleanse and bandage his scraped knees? But now he is beyond my reach. I can only follow and watch helplessly. I stagger on, more determined with every step to be near him.

When we are overcome by burdens, let us remember that, lying there on the ground, Jesus came to know and would always understand our powerlessness. Jesus' way to Calvary is all about his love for us then, his love for us now, his mercy, and the gift of life we have in him.

The Fourth Station: Jesus Meets His Mother

As I push and shove to move through the crowds to be as close to my Son as I can, we come to a place in the road where he stops. He sees me. And we look into each other's eyes. I don't want him to see my tears or know my pain, but I long ago accepted how thoroughly he knows me. I pour my love into this touchless embrace. My lips quietly say the prayer he taught us: "Father, may your Kingdom come and your will be done on earth as it is in heaven." He nods so slightly, takes a deep breath, and moves on up the hill.

Jesus has tasted the separation and loss that every person in the world who has lost a loved one knows. He has understood the heart of every loving mother who grieves at the suffering of her children. He has become so completely one with us.

The Fifth Station: Simon Helps Jesus Carry His Cross

Can't you see that he is unable to go on, carrying the cross alone? Who will help him? Oh, the guard grabs someone and forces him to help Jesus: it is Simon! My relief is mixed with worry for this good man.

Let us give thanks that Jesus entered into our lives. In this gesture of help, Jesus came to know the experience of all of us who must depend upon others, for we cannot make it alone.

Let us pause for a moment to express to him now whatever is in our hearts.

The Sixth Station: Veronica Wipes the Face of Jesus

Blood and sweat mix with spit, and bruises and swelling distort his beloved face. I can hardly recognize his features. Suddenly, out of the crowd, a woman pushes past the Roman soldiers and wipes his face with her veil. Oh, how I love her for that! Her courage and compassion touch me deeply. I look at the veil, and there is a stunning likeness of Jesus's face imprinted on it.

Remember, this true icon is the face of solidarity with all who have ever experienced abuse and violence, a sign of his solidarity with us in every aspect of our lives.

140

The Seventh Station: Jesus Falls the Second Time

He falls again. My heart sinks as he stumbles and crumples to the ground. I can feel the jarring pain through my whole body. Helpless to help him, I pray.

When we suffer from any kind of physical disease that weakens us, when we must confront the limits of our bodies, we can always turn to Jesus for understanding and comfort.

With gratitude in our hearts, we take a few moments to find the words to express our feelings to him.

The Eighth Station: Jesus Meets the Women of Jerusalem

How does he have the strength to speak to the women in the crowd? He must have heard their weeping and lamentation. His words are loud enough that I can catch the warning in them, the prophecy of what is yet to come. Oh, how many

times were we stunned by his teaching: the authority with which he delivered his message, the turn of phrase that caught the ear and snagged our imagination, and the conviction behind his words. Even now, on this road of sorrow, he urges us to look beyond the present. Yet, my dear Son, how can I not weep for you?

Jesus, the rabbi, is our teacher, too. In baptism, we are signed to be priest, prophet, and king. Let us reflect on the ways that the encounter with his suffering, death, and resurrection helps us respond to the challenges of life.

The Ninth Station: Jesus Falls the Third Time

His steps are unsteady, his knees are buckling, and blood is streaking down his torso as he collapses again. My heart stops, for he is not moving; he just lies there, face in the dirt, his arms spread out. Oh God of Israel, is this the end?

Is he dead? My cries are muffled as I turn my face into my head covering to shut out the horrible sight. Grant me courage to stay with him, O God!

Contemplating how the soldiers roughly pulled Jesus up and made him take the last steps to Calvary, let us take a few moments to speak with him, expressing our gratitude for his understanding of every weakness or failure we have ever experienced.

The Tenth Station: Jesus Is Stripped

Is there no end to their cruelty? They strip him naked, exposing to the gaze of all this body that I have bathed and cared for. Their rough handling reopens his wounds.

Jesus is united with all the people in the world who are vulnerable and without any defense, all those whose dignity is violated, and those who suffer.

The Eleventh Station: Jesus Is Nailed to the Cross

I stop my ears, but the sound of metal ringing against metal penetrates anyway. I cannot look, just stand there, horrified, my stomach roiling. As my vision fades, I recall the wood splinters I pulled from his fingers, his gentle touch that healed so many, and his arms around me. Those arms are now stretched out, wide open, embracing all.

Spend some time with him now, let Jesus embrace you.

The Twelfth Station: Jesus Dies on the Cross

I feel the pain coursing through him with every attempt to breathe. If I could, I would take away all his suffering. My companions and I are standing closer now. He still whispers words of mercy and love when all I feel is pain and the anger of helplessness. With his last breath, the floodgates open, and I hear myself keening with the others.

At the foot of his cross today, listen to Jesus tell you of his love for you. Speak to him from your heart.

The Thirteenth Station: Jesus Is Taken Down from the Cross

How long before we can take his lifeless body off that cross?

He had been given to me for only a brief time. When he left home three years ago, I was so proud of him and excited to experience what God would do through him. Here at the foot of the cross, my heart is torn by grief. I cling to God's promise to lift up the lowly, and I pray for the strength to go on.

When grief and sorrow weigh you down, remember that the cross is not the end of the story. God's faithfulness is the basis of our hope and trust. In Jesus, God's love became incarnate.

The Fourteenth Station: Jesus Is Laid in the Tomb

No mother should ever have to bury a child. And no mother should have to do it in haste. We scramble to wrap Jesus's body and take him to the tomb that was offered for our use. There is no time to pray over him, shedding tears and wailing in grief. I have to leave him. As the stone is rolled in place, my heart is sealed in the tomb.

As we picture this scene, let us place the image of the empty tomb before our eyes.

Whenever you are tempted to stand outside any tomb and grieve, remember this empty tomb and know that, through the eyes of faith, all tombs are empty.

Today, give thanks to Jesus.

In the name of the Father and of the Son and of the Holy Spirit. Amen.

—Agnes Kovacs

—*An Easter Prayer*—

Almighty and everlasting God, who has vouchsafed the Paschal Mystery in the covenant of our reconciliation, grant unto our souls that what we celebrate by our profession we may imitate in our practice. Through Jesus Christ our Lord.

—GREGORIAN SACRAMENTARY[18]

—*Prayer for Easter*—

The Lord of life has risen with power,
    bringing with him love and justice,
    respect, forgiveness, and reconciliation.
The One who from nothingness
    had called the world into existence,
    only he could break the seals of the tomb,
    only he could become the source of New Life.

—POPE ST. JOHN PAUL II[19]

—*Christ is Risen!*—

Christ is risen from the dead!
He is risen as he said!
Christ the firstborn dies no more,
Christ our Shepherd! Christ the Door.
By his cross he set us free.
Christ himself, our victory!
Alleluia! God be praised!
Alleluia! Christ is raised!

—HARRY HAGAN, OSB[20]

—*Pentecost*—

Grant, Almighty God, that we who celebrate the solemnity of the gift of the Holy Spirit, may be kindled with heavenly desires and thirst for the fountain of life. Through Jesus Christ our Lord.

—GREGORIAN SACRAMENTARY[21]

—*Prayer for Faithfulness*—

O God, who was pleased to send your Holy Spirit, the Paraclete, in the burning fire of your love, grant to your people to be fervent in unity of faith; that evermore abiding in you, they may be found both steadfast in faith and active in work. Through Jesus Christ, our Lord.

—GELASIAN SACRAMENTARY[22]

—*Prayer for Illumination*—

May the Spirit, the Paraclete, O Lord, who proceeds from you, illuminate our minds, and, as your Son had promised, lead us into all truth. Through the same our Lord Jesus Christ.

—GELASIAN SACRAMENTARY[23]

—*Prayer for the Gifts and Fruits of the Holy Spirit*—

Give me, O Lord, purity of lips, a clean and innocent heart, and rectitude in action.

Give me humility, patience, abstinence, chastity, prudence, justice, fortitude, temperance.

Give me the Spirit of wisdom and understanding, the Spirit of counsel and strength, the Spirit of knowledge and godliness, and of your fear.

Make me ever to seek your face with all my heart, all my soul, all my mind;

Grant me to have a contrite and humbled heart in your presence—to prefer nothing to your love.

Most high, eternal, ineffable Wisdom, drive away from me the darkness of blindness and ignorance;

Most high and eternal Strength, deliver me;

Most high and eternal Fortitude, assist me;

Most high and incomprehensible Light, illuminate me;

Most high and infinite Mercy, have mercy on me.

—GALLICAN SACRAMENTARY[24]

—Trinity—

May the infinite and glorious Trinity, the Father, the Son, and the Holy Spirit, direct our life in good works, and after our passage through this world, grant to us eternal rest with the righteous. Grant this, O Eternal and Almighty God. Amen.

—MOZARABIC MISSAL [25]

—Communion Prayer—

Son of the living God,
Lord Jesus Christ,
whose death
willed by the Father, empowered by the Holy Spirit,
restored the life of the world,
deliver me from all my iniquities and from every evil,
keep me always close to your commandments
and never allow me to be separated from you.

—9TH CENTURY PRAYER [26]

—Sancti, Venite (Come, Holy Ones)—

Draw near and take the body of the Lord,
and drink the holy blood for you outpoured.

Saved by that body and that holy blood,
with souls refreshed, we render thanks to God.

Humanity is ransomed from eternal loss
by flesh and blood offered upon the cross.
Offered was he for greatest and for least,
Himself the Victim, himself the Priest.

He that his saints in this world rules and shields
To all believers life eternal yields.
He feeds the hungry with the bread of heaven
And living streams to those who thirst are given.

Approach you then with faithful hearts sincere,
And take the pledges of salvation here.

—7ᵀᴴ CENTURY IRISH PRAYER

—Anima Christi—

Soul of Christ, sanctify me.
Body of Christ, save me.
Blood of Christ, inebriate me.
Water from the side of Christ, wash me.
Passion of Christ, strengthen me.
O good Jesus, hear me.
Within your wounds conceal me.
Do not permit me to be parted from you.
From the evil foe protect me.
At the hour of my death call me.
And bid me come to you,
to praise you with all your saints
for ever and ever.
Amen.

—Prayer for Unity—

O God, who has taught your Church to keep all your heavenly commandments by loving you and our neighbor, grant us the spirit of peace and grace, that your universal family may be both devoted to you with their whole heart, and united to each other with a pure will. Through Jesus Christ, our Lord.

—POPE LEO THE GREAT[27]

—Prayer for Divine Care—

Lord, God Almighty, Christ the King of glory, you are our true peace, and Love eternal;
enlighten our souls with the brightness of your peace, and purify our consciences with the sweetness of your love, that we may, with peaceful hearts, wait for the Author of peace, and in the adversities of this world may ever have you for our guardian and protector; and so being fenced about by your care, may heartily give ourselves to the love of your peace.

—MOZARABIC MISSAL[28]

—Prayer for Peace—

To the Creator of nature and humankind, of truth and beauty, I pray:

Hear my voice, for it is the voice of the victims of all wars and violence among individuals and nations.

Hear my voice, for it is the voice of all children who suffer and will suffer when people put their faith in weapons and war.

Hear my voice when I beg You to instill into the hearts of all human beings the wisdom of peace, the strength of justice, and the joy of fellowship.

Hear my voice, for I speak for the multitudes in every country and in every period of history who do not want war and are ready to walk the road of peace.

Hear my voice and grant insight and strength so that we may always respond to hatred with love, to injustice with total dedication to justice, to need with the sharing of self, to war with peace.

O God, hear my voice and grant unto the world Your everlasting peace.

—POPE ST. JOHN PAUL II[29]

—Prayer for Guidance—

Bless all who worship you, almighty God, from the rising of the sun to its setting: from your goodness enrich us, by your love inspire us, by your Spirit guide us, by your power protect us, in your mercy receive us, now and always.

—ANCIENT COLLECT

—The Divine Praises—

Blessed be God.

Blessed be his Holy Name.

Blessed be Jesus Christ, true God and true man.

Blessed be the name of Jesus.

Blessed be his most Sacred Heart.

Blessed be his most Precious Blood.

Blessed be Jesus in the most Holy Sacrament of the Altar.

Blessed be the Holy Spirit, the Paraclete.

Blessed be the great Mother of God, Mary most holy.

Blessed be her holy and Immaculate Conception.

Blessed be her glorious Assumption.

Blessed be the name of Mary, virgin and mother.

Blessed be Saint Joseph, her most chaste spouse.

Blessed be God in his angels and in his Saints.

(Optional) May the heart of Jesus, in the most Blessed Sacrament, be praised, adored, and loved with grateful affection, at every moment, in all the tabernacles of the world, even to the end of time. Amen.

—All Saints' Day—

Almighty and Everlasting God, who enkindled the flame
of your love in the hearts of the saints, grant to our minds
the same faith and power of love; that as we rejoice in their
triumphs, we may profit by their examples. Through Jesus
Christ, our Lord. Amen.

—GOTHIC MISSAL[30]

—Prayer for All the Faithful Departed—

Merciful Father,

On this day, we are called to remember those who have
   died,
Particularly those who have died in the past year,
And pray for their joyful reunion with you, their loving
   creator.
As your Son taught us to call the stranger
neighbor, our fallen are many—

Names we will never know,
Voices we have never heard,
In lands we may never visit,
Yet, brothers and sisters all.
And so we pray.

For victims of war, caught in the crossfires of
conflicts we could not quell,
for soldiers and civilians,
adults and children, we pray . . .
Grant eternal rest, O Lord.

For those migrants who have died seeking a
haven where they hoped to find safety
and opportunity for themselves and for their families,
we pray . . .
Grant eternal rest, O Lord.

For victims of hunger, denied their share in the bounty
you have placed before us, we pray . . .
Grant eternal rest, O Lord.

For victims of AIDS, Malaria, Ebola, and other infectious
  diseases,
who died before adequate care could reach them,
  we pray . . .
Grant eternal rest, O Lord.

For those refugees seeking asylum from war,
who died in a land that was not their home, we pray . . .
Grant eternal rest, O Lord.

For victims of emergencies and calamities everywhere,
who died amid chaos and confusion, we pray . . .
Grant eternal rest, O Lord.

Lord, as you command, we reach out to the fallen.

We call on you on behalf of those we could not reach this year.

You raised your Son from the dead

that all may share in his joyful resurrection.

In Jesus' name, we pray . . .

Requiem aeternam dona eis, Domine,

Et lux perpetua luceat eis.

Requiescant in pace.

Amen.

—GENEVIEVE JORDAN LASKEY, CATHOLIC RELIEF SERVICES[31]

161

—Te Deum—

You are God: we praise you;
You are the Lord: we acclaim you;
You are the eternal Father:
All creation worships you.

To you all angels, all the powers of heaven,
Cherubim and Seraphim, sing in endless praise:
    Holy, holy, holy, Lord God of hosts!
    Heaven and earth are full of your glory.
The glorious company of apostles praise you.
The noble fellowship of prophets praise you.
The white-robed army of martyrs praise you.

Throughout the world the holy Church acclaims you:
    Father of infinite majesty,
Your true and only Son, worthy of all worship,
    and the Holy Spirit, advocate and guide.

You Christ, are the king of glory,
the eternal Son of the Father.

When you became man to set us free,
you did not spurn the Virgin's womb.

You overcame the sting of death,
and opened the kingdom of heaven to all believers.

You are seated at God's right hand in glory.
We believe that you will come and be our judge.
Come then, Lord, and help your people,
    bought with the price of your own blood,
    and bring us with your saints
    to glory everlasting.

Endnotes

1. Harry Hagan, OSB, used with permission.

2. J. Philip Newell, *Celtic Treasure: Daily Scripture and Prayer* (Grand Rapids: Eedmans, 2005), 10.

3. Selina Fitzherbert Fox, *A Chain of Prayer Across the Ages: Forty Centuries of Prayer from 2000 B.C.* (New York: Dutton, 1943), 134.

4. Lisa O. Engelhardt, used with permission.

5. Catholic Church. *The Sacramentary : Approved for Use in the Dioceses of the United States of America by the National Conference of Catholic Bishops and Confirmed by the Apostolic See* (New York: Collins World, 1974).

6. William Bright, *Ancient Collects and Other Prayers Selected for Devotional Use from Various Rituals* (Oxford: Parker, 1869), 36.

7. Ibid.

8. Linda Bieker, used with permission.

9. Richard J. Beyer, *Blessed Art Thou: A Treasury of Marian Prayers and Devotions* (Notre Dame, IN: Ave Maria Press, 1996), 132.

10. Accessed at https://udayton.edu/imri/mary/e/entrustment-mary-by-pope-john-paul-ii.php.

11. *Evangelii Gaudium*, accessed at http://w2.vatican.va/content/francesco/en/apost_exhortations/documents/papa-francesco_esortazione-ap_20131124_evangelii-gaudium.html.

12. Accessed at https://udayton.edu/imri/mary/p/prayers-of-pope-john-xxiii-to-mary.php, 9.

13. Accessed at http://nhop.ca/an-advent-prayer-henri-nouwen/.

14. Karl Rahner, SJ, *The Eternal Year* (Baltimore: Helicon, 1964), 24-26.

15. William Bright, *Ancient Collects and Other Prayers Selected for Devotional Use from Various Rituals* (Oxford: Parker, 1869), 26.

16. Accessed at http://msf-america.org/holy-family-prayers/prayers-devoted-to-the-holy-family/the-holy-family-prayer.

17. William Bright. *Ancient Collects and Other Prayers Selected for Devotional Use from Various Rituals* (Oxford: Parker 1869), 36.

18. Harry Hagan, OSB, used with permission.

19. Ibid., 56.

20. Jacquelyn Lindsey, *Catholic Family Prayer Book* (Huntington: Our Sunday Visitor, 2001), accessed at https://www.osv.com/OSVNewsweekly/Story/TabId/2672/ArtMID/13567/ArticleID/11428/Prayers-from-the-Catholic-Family-Prayer-Book.aspx#easter.

21. William Bright. *Ancient Collects and Other Prayers Selected for Devotional Use from Various Rituals* (Oxford: Parker, 1869), 62.

22. Ibid., 63.

23. Ibid.

24. Selina Fitzherbert Fox, *A Chain of Prayer Across the Ages: Forty Centuries of Prayer from 2000 B.C.* (New York: Dutton, 1943), 142.

25. William Bright. *Ancient Collects and Other Prayers Selected for Devotional Use from Various Rituals* (Oxford: Parker, 1869), 66.

26. *The Glenstal Book of Prayer* (Collegeville: Liturgical Press, 2001), 117.

27. William Bright. *Ancient Collects and Other Prayers Selected for Devotional Use from Various Rituals* (Oxford: Parker, 1869), 77.

28. Selina Fitzherbert Fox, *A Chain of Prayer Across the Ages: Forty Centuries of Prayer from 2000 B.C.* (New York: Dutton, 1943), 176.

29. Accessed at https://www.crossroadsinitiative.com/media/articles/prayers-of-pope-john-paul-ii/.

30. William Bright. *Ancient Collects and Other Prayers Selected for Devotional Use from Various Rituals* (Oxford: Parker, 1869), 69.

31. Accessed at https://www.crs.org/resource-center/all-souls-day-prayer.

About the Author

Agnes M. Kovacs, a native of Hungary, has lived in the United States for thirty years. She is a daughter, sister, aunt, wife, mother, and grandmother who cherishes the relationships with her large, extended family spanning multiple continents. Prayer, as first modeled in her family of origin and then practiced in different cultural contexts, has been a cornerstone of Agnes' life of faith. She enjoys exploring different prayer forms, both in personal and communal prayer. Agnes currently serves as director of continuing formation at Saint Meinrad Seminary and School of Theology.

Personal Reflections